Reflections

Laurie Wilkinson
The Psychy Poet

'Another masterpiece from the great man himself'

Published in UK in 2023 by BadGoose Publishing.

Copyright © Laurie Wilkinson 2023

ISBN: 9798857214497

Cover Photo: Mariana Blue

Cover Design: James Harvey.

Layout Design: James Harvey - soulsong.co.uk

Introduction

Oh my goodness another book, and now my thirteenth published in just over nine years, so still going well. For the more astute or regular among you, I should add that books ten and eleven were a bit different as book ten was a compilation of many of my humour section poems, (Laurie's Bundle of Poetic Humour). The eleventh book was a tribute to my two created lovable teddy bears Ted and Beth, with a book of all of their poems, (Tea for Two, Poetic Antics of Ted and Beth). Book twelve went back to my main published offerings of four themed sections of romance, humour, reflection and tragedy, so what is in this latest book then? Worry not for I will tell you now.

This book comes from a popular and repeated suggestion of another offering of just one theme that was fed back by positive opinion, so thus this book, "Reflections" complies with that. It contains the very best of my reflection poems from my past books, a great compendium with 78 poems included.

One presented poem, "Inner Tears" won a prestigious festival poetry competition in 2022, and very topically there is also a poem about the NHS from my recent experience of being in hospital for the very first time in all my years.

Apart from those mentioned above, the poems are examples of titles often mentioned or requested at my regular entertaining gigs, readings and presentations, with many nominated by people as their personal favourites after specifically identifying with them.

The poems presented in this book are across six section categories spanning "considerations, life, values, personal, past and tragic themes". I hope these relate to you, the reader, in reflective illustration, perhaps touching on your everyday experiences.

To help clarify my meanings of some of the poems please be aided again by my Appendix section which will explain the not so obvious topics, for I am confident that many of them will touch and resonate with you in some way as we ride the roller coaster of life together.

As ever please dive in and enjoy choosing your own favourites as "The Journey Continues" while I'm still donating to, and promoting the excellent charity Help for Heroes, that care for our wounded armed service personnel.

Thanks and Best Regards

Laurie Wilkinson Bsc (hons) RMN

Acknowledgements

This is now my thirteenth book, and with my twelfth book published under a year ago, there's still plenty of people to acknowledge!

I will start by thanking my excellent publisher and "Website Guru" James Harvey (soulsong.co.uk), alongside his patience with my "techno shortcomings" he also conjures up inspired book covers!

I have looked back over the history of all my books to recognise the "help and support" I have had which seems to fall into two main categories:

Firstly, the general advice, help, and encouragement to actually write, and secondly, the support, assistance and opportunities to promote and sell my books. Each book still donates to the excellent charity 'Help for Heroes' that cares for our armed forces wounded.

The lists of all the people involved in the two points above could be almost endless, so I will just loosely touch upon key players and organisations here, and thank the many others personally. Obviously over my nine years plus now of publication, some folks have "come and gone" in the natural movements, involvements and flow of life.

Encouraging and advising on my writing mainly have been my (now late) wife Iris, and all my family. Elizabeth Wright (The Writer) mentored and advised me from the very start and is currently still working on 'my' story.

Alongside my (often manic) efforts to promote me and my books have been Lyn Parsons of National Magic FM Radio with her endorsements, readings and mentions of me; Sylvie Blackmore of BBC Radio Sussex & Surrey who has now had me as guest on her show multiple times to read my poems and to talk about my poetry world and; Simon Herbert of Hailsham FM and Seahaven Radio F M now too for my regular guest slots, all of whom have also promoted my selected charity Help for Heroes too.

The 42nd Highland Regiment (1815) for support and buying my books; Hailsham Chamber of Commerce; The Sussex Newspaper Online for allowing my monthly column for over eight years now; Hailsham News with my monthly Poetry Corner; The Team at Tesco Langley for allowing and helping my book sales and collecting for Help for Heroes.

Local East Sussex businesses, shops, pubs, (many who sell my books particularly now Cafe Old Town Eastbourne); many charities and all the wonderful people I meet and liaise with too numerous to mention all individually by name.

I am particularly grateful to Lesley A T, a colleague from the past; Richard Williams for his advice; Geoff H & Bob "Donbo" long ago school friends; Julie A V, Debbie & Sharon B's as "The Twister Sisters" who are still my lead Quality Assurance readers. Many, many more must remain unmentioned but not forgotten as you will be thanked elsewhere and perhaps personally.

As I mentioned earlier, James Harvey who has also published this book for me under Bad Goose Publishing as he did my previous five books too, so a big thanks to him for all his help and guidance and our new ideas as I strive to continue as an increasingly prolific, determined and hopefully innovative poet and author! A great partnership I think.

As always, my final recognition of gratitude is to you people taking the time to read this book, and with an even bigger thanks to the kind folks who have bought my previous books, and buy this one too. This, as ever, ensures my donation to the excellent charity Help for Heroes from all my sales.

Thanks again, and bless you all,

Laurie

Reflection

Reflection can allow you closure
To set matters right in your head,
So perhaps allowing peace inside
And no troubled thoughts instead.

For careful considerations made
With that great gift of hindsight,
Can arrange things in perspective
And be seen in a fresher light.

So directions we may want to take
Or any successes that we yearn,
Could come about much easier now
If from reflective views we learn.

Contents

Laurie Wilkinson

CONSIDERATIONS

A Across the Way

We nearly all have a cross to bear,
They can be big, or sometimes small.
Some will have lots, others not many
Though the lucky have none at all.
So we stagger along our roads
With these burdens on our back,
Of varying degrees, each one of us
Trying to keep to the beaten track.

Some people's crosses you never see,
For they wear pain behind a mask
Of a ready smile or flippant joke,
Inside though, crushed by their task.

But others will keep telling you
How hard their life with no reward,
Despite every help they won't pass on
So will never earn happy accord.
How then I wonder is this all agreed
With life's loads unfairly shared?
And unkind people let off scot-free
When for others they never cared.

But those diamond folks of our world
Who care for everyone else first,
Will carry such a big and heavy cross
You think their heart must burst,
Though somehow they stagger on
Managing to help many foe or friend.
So you come to realise their worth
Knowing they'll win out in the end.

--ooOoo--

Recycle Plant

Zooming round his treadmill
Hammy the hamster went,
It seems he really likes it
For that's how his time is spent.
Though for all his frantic efforts
He doesn't get too far in life,
But is this so much different
From many people's world of strife?

Rushing off through their day
Crowds of people in a dash,
Getting nowhere, trying hard
To earn that bit of extra cash.
And though their chaotic world
Doesn't have the hamster's bars,
It's really not so different
As getting gridlocked in their cars!

And so in our world of wonder
We can fly to our heart's desire,
But many people's bland routine
Ensures entrapment in their mire.

Laurie Wilkinson

Thus in cages without walls
Moaning folk are sat restrained,
With all their thoughts of freedom
Yet no real effort is maintained.
For it's so easy to talk of flight
With feet planted on the ground,
Meaning that no escape or joy
From their boring world is found!

--ooOoo--

Daze End

Sitting in my favourite chair
In my most comfortable way,
Looking back at hours passed
To reflect how went the day?

Well some go very well
And others not so good,
So in the scheme of life
That must be understood.

But more important than this
Is your dealing with it all,
Smiling with the good days
And giving no cause to fall.
But what about the bad times
That can also arrive too?
Can we get up if knocked down?
May define both me and you!

So how well the day went is crucial
But our responses so much more,
For if you react to adversity
Your life will be more secure,
Than if you just roll over
Bleating about your lack of luck,
So if not standing your own ground
You may regret your lack of pluck!

--ooOoo--

All or Something

Life is a feast or famine
And never seems to even out,
Either all the land is flooding
Or we're suffering a drought.

If you want to catch a bus
You are standing like a dunce,
Past your final waiting time
Then four will come at once!

Luck seems to be the same
You will get every call right,
Then quickly as it changes
You lose everything in sight.

Getting your finances done
Bills paid with money left,
When a run of expenses come
And all at once you are bereft.

Fishermen cast their bait
And the nets are filled tight,
But then there is a long time
With not one single bite.

Life is feast or famine
And never seems to even out,
Either all the world is flooding
Or we're suffering a drought.

Is it a game that's played
By angels and mascots creed?
That allows a win sometimes
Before stopping all our greed.

Perhaps it's our perception
Of what we want to obtain.
But whatever does befall us
We must get back up again!

--ooOoo--

Loaves and Fishes

Well I can't say that I've met Jesus
But maybe some who thought they were,
And looking back on my work in Psychy
That idea did quite frequently occur.
Although actually I was thinking of those
Who seem to pull rabbits out of hats,
And defy all the laws of any reason
Without making their potions with bats.

Now I'm talking about the glib and cocky
Sort of barrow boy with all the rabbit,
Who would sell some sand to the Arabs
That for him is quite a regular habit,
Because he is that type of glib person
Who will always just say that he can,
Do everything else that others can't
But mostly it will be another scam.

For I have provided buckets of water
And asked him to turn it into wine,
Which of course he didn't want to try
Even if it would be all his, not mine.
But then he will start up once again
With his second hand car sales patter,
Knowing we really don't believe it
But to him that doesn't matter.

For his next trick or shady deal
To make him or others stinking rich,
Is really only a brief whisper away
And he's sure he will without a hitch.
But obviously now he's been rumbled
As the king of twaddle, not so chick,
So best to avoid him like the plague
And not get caught by any latest trick.

Thus it all seems so very sad now
As he can't conjure up loaves and fishies,
But will continue to stay and annoy us
Despite all our prayers and wishes.

--ooOoo--

Please Ring the Bell

Being a frequent observer of life
I commit scenes and ideas to verse,
So any of my interpreting thoughts
Will reflect the better or worse.

Thus recently I had an occasion
With a situation right before me,
For when having tea in a cafe
A whole situation I could see,
Because the tea room was busy
And staff dealing with the orders,
Often leaving the desk unattended
If held up by attention hoarders.

There was though on a counter
In clear view so you could tell,
A polite notice saying for service
Please ring this alerting bell.

Now this caused some consternation
With some people reluctant to act,
And ding the bell for some attention
For a boldness they clearly lacked.
Whilst other folks had no concerns
To ring the bell with a firm hand,
So everyone working in the place
Could hear it and understand.

Now others tried to just ignore
The need of the bell to ring,
And so looked behind the counter
Hoping attention it would bring.
But of more amusement to me
At my grandstand view so clear,
Were people striding forth firmly
To ring for all hell to hear.

So all in all it was an education
Of human nature on display,
How different people will react
To a simple task on the day.
Showing the nervous and timid
Opposed to the confident and strong,
Who probably confront their life
Believing they can never be wrong.

--ooOoo--

An Inside Job

On a night of non stirring air
With anonymous perfection,
That's the time to sit and deal
With deeds that need correction.

For any self doubt or sorrow
And a pain that never goes,
Has to be sorted, or put right,
Or it like a cancer grows.

But running away or hiding
Was not the way to solve,
Problems hid, or still denied
Should that be your resolve.

How could you ever run away
Or leave others all deceived?
When you know for certain sure
You will never be believed.

So best for heartfelt honesty
On that night of non stirring air,
With its anonymous perfection
You must be forced to dare,
To tear off all that armour
Which protects the unseen you,
And come to terms with feelings
That on your inside grew!

--ooOoo--

Conspiracy

Just another doubting Thomas
Or maybe a pressure group belief,
That things didn't actually happen
Perhaps lied about through teeth,
That were firmly clenched closed
In an effort to keep in the lie,
About just what really did occur
With how, when and why?

For there are many conspiracy theories
On what actually had occurred
Because people refuse to believe in,
Any explanations or the word,
That says just what has happened
And in this or that manner.
But many people won't accept it
And hoist their doubting banner.

For lots of folks who won't accept
There was ever a moon landing,
Have various queries and disagree
With the story that is still standing,
Relating to a successful mission
To win first man on moon race,
For the conspiracy groups believe
It was a huge lie and disgrace.

Other doubts and questions cover
The twin towers attack event,
And the disappearance of Shergar
With all the money that was spent,
Trying to find him, and hasn't yet
Been resolved, whatever is now said.
And of course there are still those
Who don't think that Elvis is dead.

In history a strange story of a ship
That's shrouded in myth and mystery,
And loads of theories and guesses
On the Marie Celeste drifting at sea.

Another very long running debate
Which says no facts are crystal clear,
And that none of our great plays
Were really written by Shakespeare.
Also there's an unsolved mystery
That surrounds the Lord Lucan case.
Who suspiciously just vanished,
Some allege to save guilty face.

Though looking at huge controversies
And constant accusations of a lie,
Surrounds the mysterious tragic death
Of the very popular Lady Di.
Along with a callous assassination
Of President Kennedy in Dallas City,
Where theory arguments still rage
And very little signs of pity.

Flying saucers are regularly seen
But with no confirmations to explain,
Why circles in crop fields had appeared
So doubts and worries still remain.
Thus on and on debates will go
As conspiracy ideas continue to sprout,
For however mysteries are viewed
There will always be some doubt.

--ooOoo--

Yellow Brick Code

The yellow brick road is attractive
And can lead to all your dreams,
But beware what is too easy
It's not always how it seems.
Often leading to more heartache
That you ever felt could befall,
With crushed lives and sadness
And best intentions beyond recall.

So you set off on your journey
With scant care or backward look,
To follow a path to promised wonder
But sadly a wrong turn you took.
No pearly path led to your hopes
Or road to make a life fulfil
With no escape to a crowning glory,
Instead it all just made you ill!

You felt you had all the trump cards
And your win was the certain tip,
But it's always as well to remember
That dreaded slip "twixt cup and lip".
For it's not what you have that's crucial
But your use and mastery of skills,
For it's about the singer, not the song
And how well you learn the drills.

No sanctuary can now placate you
From all that chagrins hurt inside,
For however hard you try to twist it
You just gave away your pride.
So best to try now and enjoy the chaos
Brought about by the selfish needs,
Sadly no yellow brick road for you
Only shame for sad callous deeds.

--ooOoo--

Laurie Wilkinson

Alone in the Mirror

I am alone in the mirror
With this face I've come to know,
That's been staring back at me
From so many years ago.
But that face has changed now
Though the expression is the same,
For it has seen much of life
And situations you can't tame.

This face has looked on loss
So tragic it creased with pain,
While trying hard to smile out
As inside the heart was slain.
Inner traumas rocked the soul
Which nearly split the seam.
Causing untold agony but,
Outside the face would beam.

So laughter which we cherish
Has cracked the outer look,
Though these smile fed lines
Can belie the times it shook,
With mirth, and sometimes grief
As it was worn across the years,
That eroded pristine youth
With many of life's fears.

So that cruel mirror on my wall
Reflects the good and bad,
Showing with lines and wrinkles
All the years of life I've had.
But I'm not ashamed of this
Please don't be taken in.
For though sometimes I force it,
Years drop off when I grin.

--ooOoo--

Laurie Wilkinson

A Throw of the Dice

Lured and beguiled by temptations net
We may hear sirens alluring sounds,
For responses wake excited feelings
As our heartbeat skips and pounds.

Thus again loves trap is baited
For times that can be very nice,
So take that moment of reflection
Before any rolling of the dice.
For the lure of promised pleasure
With a gorgeous sight of wonder,
Blinds any awareness sighted
So with our dice we blunder.

Oh, but there is brief satisfaction
And ecstasy to make you smile,
Though make the very most of it
As it will only last a while,
Before reality and acceptance call
To tell you of impending fate,
As you took a chance on rolling dice
So now it is too late.

For a moment you may look back
And consider what has been done,
Because the light is dawning now
That you have nowhere left to run,
As the dye is now finally cast
Just as you did with those dice,
And now regretting your deaf ears,
On all that good advice.

So just where have you landed,
And what will happen now?
Well, you still have a brief chance
Thus it's best to make your bow,
For you gave into temptation
Ignoring what friends had to say.
Now sadly you will remember,
About the dog who had his day!

--ooOoo--

One Voice

I woke to the disappointment
Of rain hammering my mobile home,
For a storm seemed right overhead
And was pounding the roof dome.
So I turned over and back to sleep
To awake again in another hour,
But sadly the rain had not ceased
And thus my mood was sour.

But lying in bed hearing the din
A minor miracle then occurred,
For against the noise on my roof
Came the sweet singing of a bird.
A solitary chirping of morning joy
From a little chap I couldn't see,
But the song he continually sang
Was a great delight to me.

Though what had motivated this bird
Whose song beat the noisy rain,
I'm sure I will never really know
But he kept up with his refrain.
Now I'm no great bird expert
So couldn't tell the type or family,
But because he sang out in a storm
His form I didn't need to see.

For soon a couple of other birds
Joined in with the singular voice,
Maybe encouraged and led by him
Or perhaps just their own choice.

So now against a strong backdrop
Of rain clattering on my roof,
I had this wonderful little choir
Singing out in beautiful proof,
That even in our dismal times
A determined song by one voice,
Can overcome depressive scenes
To offer a happier choice.

--ooOoo—

Bridges

A bridge can join two sides up
But if destroyed keep them apart.
For if you need to cross a gorge
The bridge will help you start,
Bringing a joining up as one
Separate sides of an argument.
For if bridging troubled waters
You may have a hearts content.

Many people burn their bridges
So they have no safe road back,
And if they need to turn around
They will realise what they lack.
For you may need to bridge build
If some offences you have caused,
To someone who you've let down
When affections you have paused.

So a bridge can make a short cut
From a very long way around,
Although before putting faith in it
Best ensure it's safe and sound,
Or you will learn the hard way
That quickest isn't always best.
And if that route is with people
Take care to pass their test.

As like houses strong foundations
They're best built over time,
So bridges covering friendship
Must be sincere to be sublime.

For friends who last a lifetime
Will have had their rocky roads,
So the only way to survive this
Is with personal highway codes.

--ooOoo--

Laurie Wilkinson

Reflections

LIFE

Open Up

I'm so glad that I spoke to you
How else would I have known,
Thoughts that you have told me
Which are all your very own?

You shared just what you think
What makes you laugh or cry,
Some things that make you angry,
That you love, or perhaps let by.

Now we can often pass each other
Without a smile or spoken word,
And that we don't talk to each other
Is quite frankly so absurd.

We need to share our feelings
And how others may endure.
For in a world of madness
It's good to know what's pure.
By listening and talking
We learn some different views,
Like how life can be for others
When before we had no clues.

Laurie Wilkinson

Now we can often pass each other
Without a smile or spoken word,
And that we don't talk to each other
Is quite frankly so absurd.

So give a nod, or even smile
Who knows what may pan out?
You may have great times spent
If you end your speaking drought!

--ooOoo--

Hospitalisation

We know an underfunded NHS is creaking
So I did wonder a bit what I would find,
When having to be rushed into hospital
But it wasn't the main thing on my mind.
For I was in severe agony and worrying
Just what was causing my intense pain,
But on being met by an emergency doctor
I got a reassured confidence back again.

For I was soon to be looked after very well
And treated in a valued and dignified way,
Which embraced all involvements from staff
Not seemingly to falter or even sway,
From a totally caring, committed approach
And camaraderie gallows humour for events,
Testing, saddening and shredding stout hearts
But never diminished any of their intents.

Thus as I considered this new world for me
For I had never been in hospital before,
I was impressed by positivity and hard work
Of various team grades giving all and more,
That could be reasonably asked of them now
With staff shortages and pressure of work,
From budget cuts and paltry wage rises
Grating on levels of duty they do not shirk.

So let us not treat our NHS with impunity
Or overuse the services unless we have to,
For these overcrowded committed areas
Normally have more than enough to do.
Therefore we must do our very level best
And stay sensible and use common sense,
To be healthy and look after ourselves
So pressure on NHS is not so immense.

--ooOoo--

Will

Well weeks will come and weeks will go
And months soon follow in life's flow.
But days we enjoy will pass by quick,
Whilst tougher times go slow.

So then we must remain steadfast
With our resolve strong and unbowed,
As all of us will have our turn
To be under a sad, tragic cloud.
For nothing in this world is given
To remain the same, or even arrive.
So grab those moments of delight
And just celebrate you're alive!

There will of course be time for sorrow
With that very time going slow,
So try to cry behind your mask
Because others may not know.

Well at least that's what I try to do
Not that I think men shouldn't cry.
But I shed my tears in private
So the world doesn't puzzle why
This chap with a constant smile
And a jokes all-day token,
May continue to laugh and grin,
When inside his heart has broken.

So back we will go to the weeks
Which pass according to our fate,
But whether going quick or slow
We should retain a grateful state.

--ooOoo--

Lane Strain

The endless narrow leafy lanes
Were graced by overhanging trees too,
And were brought to a sparkling life
When sunlight lanced brightly through,
Those branches and leaves all round
Making the lanes come alive more,
But now also dangerous and restricting
The visibility making drivers unsure.

Because the combination of glaring sun
And rain-spattered, puddle filled road,
Challenged concentration and vision
Like questions from the Highway Code.
So I regularly had to slow down now
To determine just where I was going.
For flickering shadows and sunlight
Can undo the unwary or unknowing.

But apart from the over-riding strain
Of this concentrating and blinking,
Was the natural beauty of the lanes
To appreciate while steadily thinking,
About your speed and the windy road
That seemed to continue for ever.
Which may have been a pleasant scene
If wasn't for the changing weather.

So a sweet and sour journey continued
And seemingly was not having an end,
Battling both relaxing and being alert
For another surprising and sharp bend.

But it is normally right about this time
That I give an appreciation to my car,
For if ever getting confused or even lost
The techno knows just where you are.

--ooOoo--

Exposure

It takes a very brave person
To rise above the parapet alone,
And to show themselves completely
Whilst standing on their own.

Now of course they would expect
That others would support them too.
But sadly not quite the case
As some find it hard to do,
Something else for any others,
Or maybe it's indifference
That causes them to duck out
All safe behind their fence.

Of course they watch keenly
To see what happens next,
With their well rehearsed excuse
Or some other lame pretext,
That will justify themselves
From any exposure to the fray.
As they really do believe it's best
To run, and fight another day.

So what of our poor victim
Now standing open to it all?
Leading a flock who didn't follow,
And maybe smile to see him fall.
For in some cases it would suit
The cowards to say, I told you so.
We were right to keep our cover
And thus not to have a go.

Which certainly would be safer
And not take any chance to gain
Successful wins in their life,
But all their fears remain.

--ooOoo--

Love to Live

To love is to live
In all things, they say,
As to feel like this
Must enrich every day.

Though some people can't,
Get love past themselves.
And the result of this is
They're left on the shelves.

Others spend their love
All on one single thing,
Which if it goes wrong
Only heartache will bring.

You can love what you do
To give you much pleasure.
So long as it's spread out,
And in equal measure.

Because I've always found
In life with kith and kin,
You get back joy and love
The more that you put in.

Laurie Wilkinson

Many folks type of love
Will only bring strife,
But for me it's all simple,
I just love my life!

--ooOoo--

Blackboard

A blackboard will often be full
Of lots of questions for you,
But if you are very fortunate
It will have the answers too.

So the blackboard can educate
By stretching out your mind,
And also solving the problems
If the answers you can't find.
Which is all complete in a lesson
And maybe an end time as well,
That gives you a confidence
As you feel knowledge swell.

But sadly life is not like this
With everything spoon fed right,
For the world will often test us
And dump from a great height.
So we may be totally rocked
Wondering what is going on,
As we are further stressed out
Before disasters are all gone.

Therefore we must quickly learn
How to deal with life's downside,
And gird our loins to fight back
Rather than to run and hide.

For if we can withstand all of
Those harsh lessons of dark days,
Without the help of a blackboard
It will ensure our courage stays.

--ooOoo--

Ricochet

A ricochet is a rebound
Not arriving where intended,
Often hitting someone by mistake
And not so easily mended.

For the person hit or injured
Still feels the same pain,
As if they were aimed at
But are lucky they're not slain.
So whether an actual missile
Or an angry spoken word,
Wasn't meant for the victim
The suffering is real and heard.

For sadly in everyday lives
We get more than we can take,
So if we explode and lash out
Our outburst has no brake,
Should we see it's badly aimed
And heading in a wrong direction.
Which causes distress and regret
At the lack of aimed perfection.

It can also be the same with love
And relationships on a rebound,
That is also a form of ricochet
If a true love isn't found.

So it's probably best to take time
And make certain our aim is sure,
Because even Cupid gets it wrong
Which can only lead to more,
Heartache, hurt and upset
Firing off without a thought.
Which causes pain and anguish
If careless revenge is sought.

--ooOoo--

Cowboys and Motorists

In those days of the wild west
People all travelled around by horse,
Mostly riding on these animals
With coaches and carts of course.

So I wonder how it would all go
If we drove about like on horseback,
And substituted cars into that wild west
Maybe having to repel an Indian attack?
Would our vehicles cope with that terrain
Or lots of horses fit well in the city?
But I don't think we can ever see this
So in some ways that's a pity.

For many motorists driving behaviour
Lends itself to those lawless days,
Seen in the old western towns
Riding their horses in careless ways.

Though of course back in that rough time
Horses were not subject to body repair,
And with any little coming together
Nobody would just get off and stare,
To see if any damage for insurance
Which could land you up in court,
And possibly a more perilous ending
Than who was the driver at fault.

As maybe it would have been settled
By both parties going for their gun,
So one of them might be killed
Or be left lying out in the sun.
Thus not for them any third parties
With any witness statement need,
To ensure that justice was done
And the innocent would succeed.

But alas although we've moved on
From horseback to modern car.
Some still drive as if on the plains
When any street courtesy is far
Away from their immediate thought,
Which is to complete their drive
In the shortest time that's possible,
And just hope they stay alive.

Thus I would like to now see
Modern day sheriffs on our roads,
To monitor and punish rash cowboys
And enforce the highway codes.

--ooOoo--

I Hope it Doesn't Rain

At last everything is organised
With only a brief little pain,
And just one thing we can't control
So let's hope it doesn't rain.

For downpours have the ability
To literally put a damper on things,
However much all else is done
Any wet weather certainly brings,
Some slowing down or even stop
To all festivities that are planned.
So without a chance of recourse
Rain can take things out of hand.

For however we try to be stalwarts
And put on a brave, happy face,
Staying indoors to avoid the rain
Is really no great disgrace,
For the busy crowd hoped for
Will be that significantly less.
As slopping about in wet and mud
Just causes great distress.

So "I really hope it doesn't rain",
Is a regular offered up saying.
Because of all the consequences
So no wonder you are praying,
To have a pleasant weather day
Even if it's dry and very cold.
For we can deal with this
And see the intrepid and bold.

But rain can really ruin the day
Making everything all wet,
So I hope it doesn't rain at all
And a dry sunny day we get.

--ooOoo--

Laurie Wilkinson

Lists

I have to write out my lists
And use them all the time,
So that I don't forget things
As no longer in my prime.

But hang on, that isn't fair
As this is no new thing I do,
For if I stop to think about it
I've always written quite a few,
Because often just the one list
Is insufficient for the day,
So I have lists to remember lists
Or else thoughts may go away.

So yes, sometimes I have three
Different reminders for my brain,
And on occasions even four
But that's quite hard to explain.

So what do these notes consist of
That requires putting onto paper?
Well there are ongoing things
Or for my next shopping caper,
Where I wander with my trolley
Clutching my precious little list,
To collect all the things I want
And ensure lapses don't exist.

Some lists are household chores
Or various journeys I must make,
To guarantee all is safely done
And prevent a memory mistake.
For though I'm highly organised
Things can still get missed,
So to prevent this I write down
To go and check my other list.

--ooOoo--

Laurie Wilkinson

Darkness

Some people don't like the dark
Others it just makes scared,
But there can be a comfort too
If all your soul you've bared.

Turning out the night time bulb
As if the power has all blown,
Can put you in a covering veil
Like in some protected zone.

Tired eyes will have their rest
And an aching body its ease,
So you can be lost in yourself
Where no one has the keys.

Many people cannot cope with this
It releases all their fears,
Some with recent broken hearts
Will collapse in flooding tears.
For any aching of the soul
Will damage the weak and brittle,
Leaving them all knocked about
Just as if they were a skittle.

But I can be at one with dark
So long as I have a beam,
To turn on if I feel the need
For I like my dark fed dream.

This takes away the daytime trials
Which can leave us all aggrieved,
Thus slipping into my warm dark
My soul will feel relieved.

--ooOoo--

Laurie Wilkinson

Who Goes There?

Remembering passwords is hard
And also a user name too,
Before gaining any access
On technology owned by you.

But you tap in with a confidence
The word needed to log in,
Though sadly it comes up "error"
For this battle you won't win.
So you try again, so sure you're right
By putting in your word name.
This will surely be the one
But the failure's just the same.

"Forgotten your password?" flashes up
And through gritted teeth you hiss,
"No of blooming course not"
I just like playing this
Stupid and annoying game,
Before I can check my screen
And read all my information,
Though it looks like I'm too keen!

Change your password on here then
And all will be right for you,
But you will need to add your
User name, before this you do,
And successfully pass this test,
That's now making you see red.
So you bash your keys in anger
And watch the screen go dead.

"Oh most holy gosh and bother"
You mutter under your breath,
Knowing that it's all your fault
That caused the lap top's death.
For it doesn't want to respond
Whatever trick you try to use,
So it seems like poetic justice
If technology you abuse.

A journey to the repairers
Is now a trip you must make,
Confessing or not your guilt
You had more than you could take,
In dealing with requirements
Of all security names and text,
That you thought would be easy
But you forgot what came next.

Laurie Wilkinson

So if there is an answer to all this
And to not look like a clown,
It's to say bugger their advice
And write your passwords down!

--ooOoo--

Reflections

Laurie Wilkinson

VALUES

The Friend

Strong is the friend who stands by you
When others turn aside,
Soon as they're asked to help
They are off to run and hide.

True is the friend who stands by you
In times of your demise,
Always there to chat and cheer
To make sense of all the lies.

Humble is the friend who stands by you
And can't see what he's done
By being right alongside you
With no thought to cut and run.

Loyal is the friend who stands by you
Even if he feels you're wrong,
And tries to mediate a deal
To leave you standing strong.

Caring is the friend who stands by you
When all blows up in your face,
Then will resolve and tend your hurt
And play down the disgrace.

Laurie Wilkinson

What have you done to earn this friend
And who shelters from the fame?
I suspect that when he was down
You stood by them just the same!

--ooOoo--

Effortless

The Bluebells in the woods
Proclaim the coming time of spring.
And all hopes for a bright new year
With masses of joy to bring
To your celebratory table,
Laid out for the greatest feast
Consumed by all, but especially,
Those who contribute the least.

Sawdust can clog up the works
Whilst bullshit can baffle brains.
So ensure your mind is clear
And that all the rubbish drains
From the well oiled machinery,
Running in clockwork perfection.
Thus no action or effort is required
To improve or make correction.

Bees and butterflies seem to dance
As they go about their work,
With a gusto and involvement
That many would try to shirk,
Although ensuring that for them
A lion's share is obtained,
Without a hint of conscience
That in the effort they abstained.

So round and round spins the world
And fortune just a random prize,
Though often only gained by those
Who never care, or tries
To look out for any others,
Only what will affect them.
They believe that no one noticed
But watching eyes condemn.

--ooOoo--

Even Out

The roller coaster ride of life
Will test us one and all,
Just when you think you've won
That's the very time you'll fall.

So up you get and start again
Sorry, but perhaps much wiser,
To continue on your road again
Having fully cleared your visor.

For it's best to see the road ahead
To ensure no fall or trip,
As without a doubt you will err
If your awareness you let slip.
Gleeful shouts you've got it right
Can only lead to sorrow,
For any complacency in this world
Will bring sadness in the morrow.

The wise man says that if you've won
And sport the victor's crown,
Be modest with people going up
You may meet them coming down!

Laurie Wilkinson

The rollercoaster ride of life
Will test us one and all,
For just when you think you've won
That's the very time you'll fall.

So take any successes in your stride
And stand proud if you should miss,
For if you have done your very best
No one can give any more than this.

--ooOoo--

The Farmer and the Magpie

The farmer works ploughing fields
And scatters good seed around,
The Magpie will not do a stroke
But takes all that can be found.

The farmer's day starts at early dawn
And he works hard all year long,
The Magpie will take from everyone
Not thinking they've done wrong.

For it seems to some people in our life
They can give no bean nor clout,
So the more that they see you put in
That bit extra they take out!

The parable of the Talents
Tells of the man who wasted
All that he was given then,
Took yours you'd not yet tasted.

So our farmer works his boots off
To provide for him and friends,
Whilst the Magpie looks slyly on
Then just squanders more and spends.
Not thinking of the workload
That farming types put in,
But for our opportunist thief
Such a commitment is a sin!

It must be some strange attitude
That allows the thief to thrive,
Off the back of others work
Like the farmer's gathered hive.

But all this doesn't matter
To our thieving Magpie's gains,
For not a jot or care has he
For ours or the farmer's pains!

--ooOoo--

For Fathers

A father is so much more than a name
For there can be a very special bond,
Between a daughter or a son
Who can grow up especially fond
Of this figure who guides them along
Those early years, and even for life,
In his attempts to love and protect
Whilst keeping them free from strife.

Because any man can become a father
It's just a simple biological fact,
But to become a proper father and dad
There has to be a very committed pact
Of love, care and a deep devotion
Which may not always seem returned.
Although constant unconditional love
Can ensure magic rewards are earned.

Now I was fortunate to have a father
Both dedicated and also a great friend.
And thus appreciated all of our times,
So precious, and almost without end
Around my happy and witty role model
Teaching lessons I would never forget,
Because this special relationship shared,
We would never cheat on, or regret.

Now I'm quite sure I've passed that on
To the treasured gift of my son,
Who didn't always seem to comply
Even at times targeting me for fun,
In his jokes and childish pranks
But as he matured he cast that aside.
So my heart swells when he now says
That he looks on me with pride.

Thus please indulge your dear old dad
Who will do so much for you,
For it can be a lonely world without him
And that's a sad fact, but very true.
So whether it is those special times
Or maybe an incredible hobby taught,
Ensure you enjoy those precious moments
For a father's love just can't be bought.

--ooOoo--

Mirrored Image

People often say the very opposite
To what they seem to mean,
But mostly we've had reflections
That they don't want seen.

Because you cannot hide a lie
Or an inverted word or two.
As fleetingly, or more defined,
We will all see the real you.

But don't worry if you're unaware
That we all act out most days.
Although some are much better
Which means their image stays,
For that brief moment longer
Though will just as certainly go.
When in the spotlight they reflect
And then stark naked show.

But not an open kind of nudity,
Well in this scene definitely not,
For you may save that from everyone
But we've seen all else you've got,
However hard you try to hide
Those inner thoughts we all own.
So it's how we deal with truth
Especially when all alone.

So do not avoid life's mirrors
Or try too hard to conceal,
Those inner thoughts and fears
As we'll soon see what is real.

--ooOoo--

The Bloke Down The Pub

Knowledge can come from anywhere
And encyclopaedias get to the nub,
But all this pales into insignificance
Compared to the bloke down the pub.
For he will have an answer to all
Perplexing dilemmas in our world,
And with just another sip of beer
His wisdom can be unfurled.

Finance, global warning or politics
Hold no fearful concern for him,
As he preaches all the solutions
Delivered at the merest whim
Or even a pause for breath,
Well maybe just another beer,
Before he continues to reiterate
His avid rhetoric so sincere.

Thus many an amateur DIY fan
Has joined the home disaster club,
After following the advice given
By that bloke down the pub.
Who also gives out his information
About solid investments so clear.
But when they all failed miserably
The pub bloke was nowhere near.

But technology, history or the law
Are all easy to the bloke at the bar,
Who assures all willing listeners
His knowledge can take them far,
Well perhaps this was partly true
If only in theory and not fact.
Because on most occasions
The correct answers he lacked.

So found in many insurance offices
And filed with a red alert stub,
Will be failed compensation claims
On advice given down the pub.

--ooOoo--

Genuine

There are two groups mostly in our lives
With people that will, and those that won't,
So the one's that won't you cope with
Unlike the "say they will" who don't.

For if someone won't do something
However much you may ask,
You know just where you stand
And must then undertake that task.
But other folks will gladly fawn
When saying "leave it all to me",
So you are left high and dry
When there are no results to see.

Now we know it's easy to talk
With little action to show,
For what they have fully promised
Is likely to be a no go.
Unlike the stiff resistive
Who just prefer to take no part,
As they have a selfish side
With no interest to even start.

So give to me a stalwart
Who will spend life trying
To succeed and really help you,
Without a thought of lying,
About what they have to do
Despite hardship and a test.
So you will have to admire them
As they always do their best.

--ooOoo--

A Grain of Sand

A grain of sand, or a drop in the ocean
May be enough to cause commotion,
If brought together in one large amount
They can be big enough to make it count.
Because small or singles can be ignored
However many times they implored,
To get their point and views across
So are left staring at another loss.

For at most times in this cynical world
The tiny voice is lost until unfurled,
With the back up of a loud vast choir
That lift their voices so much higher,
And get all those points of view heard
With a collective singing of the word.
Just like the raging waters of a flood,
Which can harm both flesh and blood.

So be very wary of the seemingly small
Who could in years grow very tall,
And that little dog when just a pup
May really scare you when it grows up.
Thus one single grain of that fine sand
May have the ability to form a band,
Of determined people raising a voice
Into a storm that removes your choice.

Thus have a care before ignoring those
With a message and simple clothes,
As they may have the ability to dress
In uniform with others to bring distress,
That you may find very hard to take
When realising your big mistake,
In not seeing strength and mighty hand
Of drops of water and grains of sand!

--ooOoo--

Relay Race

A relay race is a team event
Consisting of races split into laps,
Run individually by team members
Who set off in staggered gaps,
So that all the participants,
Must run to waiting team mates
And pass a baton over to them,
Who then contest the race fate.

Obviously exchanging the baton
Is a crucial part of the race,
Because the speedier it is done
Will ensure the team's faster pace.
So the receiving person then sets off
On the next stage of the race trip.
But great care must be taken
Not to let the baton fall or slip.

For now we can clearly see
A relay race is not just about one
Specific team member over others,
For tactics may decide how it's run.
As some runners may be faster
But will still rely on the rest,
As important in the team effort,
When they try to be the best.

This then reminds me of our lives
When sometimes we need friends,
To stand by us and to help out
So all our heartache mends.
Thus just like the relay race
It's all a joint effort at times,
To get along lifetime roads
And find some happy climes.

So interactions are very important
With other people met on the way,
Just like the subtle baton change
Human greetings can make our day.
Thus be very conscious at all times
How important it is to share,
Fellowship and courteous behaviours
And win races when we care.

--ooOoo--

What a Piece of …..

The wonderfully expansive Shakespeare
Wrote magnificent words on everything,
From loves joy, sadness to tragedy
Using words that made hearts sing.

One such speech and quote from Hamlet
Is "what a piece of work is man",
Going on to exult, but question
As to why man kills all he can.
With the murder of animals for gain
And shredding world treasure to the bone.
But worse than this is man's wars
With people keen to cast the first stone.

Bombings, shooting and killings abound
In almost accepted daily news,
When man's bigotry, racism and hatred
Surfaces across our planet, and spews
Mass slaughter, pain and carnage,
Even now on Easter's religious day
Sri Lanka is decimated by bombs,
As evil scum murder their way.

Laurie Wilkinson

Oh what a piece of work is man?
Although I could answer profane,
But outrage and contemptuous disgust
Now seems is uttered in vain.
For our world drops in downward spiral
Lemming like, in a desire to die.
While in some places across the globe
A few people cry in anguish, "why"?

So maybe I can pose an answer
In that mutual respect has now gone.
A respect for man, animals and our world,
When for so many centuries joy shone.
But perhaps it's not yet all lost
As some are intent to put things right,
So I will stand alongside them until
We stop man being a piece of shite!

--ooOoo--

Fragile Flame

The candle of life is very fragile
And suddenly you can lose the flame,
If the world turns you on your head
So that nothing now seems the same,
As you battle on with a futile fight
That was almost lost before the start,
But fading pride has coerced you here
With a desperation to play your part.

So weakly and without much hope
You protect the flickering spirit of light,
Praying that this tiny, fragile beacon
Doesn't die and leave you without sight.,
Because those intruding doubts and fears
Are more disturbingly scary in the dark,
So should you lose that little puny, glow
It can release all your fears, so stark.

Now as you recognise what's happening
Like biting off more than you can chew,
As you see now how your very best
Won't be near enough to save you,
From impending downfall of all you know
And that your accepted values are not true,
When you hear the raucous voices of doubt
Gathering large and loud to mock you.

Thus feel no disgrace as you now crumple
Beneath your heavy and crushing load,
You once believed that you could resist
Before more cruel burdens were bestowed,
Upon your unprotected and lonely soul
Now flinching and whimpering for peace,
From the bombardment all aimed at you
Which you despairingly see won't cease.

--ooOoo--

A Fair Crack

We like to feel we've had a fair crack
Or even playing field and equal turn,
But life does not always work like that
However much we complain or yearn,
For the chances it appears others had
That you feel were not afforded to you,
As it can then bring about resentment
With discontented, unhappy view.

For if we've tried the same as others
And put in a very similar workload,
It's a completely natural expectation
To be equal distance down the road,
As it would be reasonable to expect
The same reward for effort and energy.
So if sadly that is not quite the case
Protests may be made by you and me.

Although often from the start of life
Privileges and favours may be sent,
For early experiences and environment
Given by benefit of birth clearly meant,
To give a better start and more quality
Over less fortunate who still work hard.
But in an uneven race across our world
They just never have the right card.

For there is now a common outcome
Not always measured by what you do,
But more a background and bearing
That can count as negative against you.
Whilst another form of great injustice
Making us feel bitter and aggrieved,
Is seeing unpleasant people do well
With good folk less awards received.

So make a covenant with yourself
To be pleasantly decent in all you try,
So can live happily in heart and soul
Meeting life with head held high.

--ooOoo--

Reflections

PERSONAL

Comings and Goings

We open lots of metaphoric doors
As we journey through our life,
But also closing many too
On those who cause us strife.

For there's happy doors and sad ones
And some possible to leave ajar,
If not needing a decision
Though best view these from afar.

So for me it's like the famous glass
That is half empty or half full,
And people are either in or out
Though some outside may pull,
On a door I shut behind them
Not wanting to be left out.
But once I have removed you
That's it, however much you shout!

For a friend or lover who betrays
Will surely do it all again,
And like the leopard with its spots
Their treachery will remain.
So if you want to turn your cheek
Don't cry out if you get hit

Whilst trying to forgive their sin
Because they never are quite fit,
To tread the same boards as you
Protesting their lesson has been learned,
Despite all the care you gave them
Your love and respect they spurned!

So never fear having to close a door
For a better one will open wide,
With brighter better people coming
To you, standing gloriously inside!

--ooOoo--

Daze End

Sitting in my favourite chair
In my most comfortable way,
Looking back at hours passed
To reflect how went the day?

Well some go very well
And others not so good,
So in the scheme of life
That must be understood.

But more important than this
Is how you deal with it all,
Smiling with those good days
With no cause to fall.

But what about the bad times
That can also arrive too?
Can we get up if knocked down
May define both me and you?

So how well the day went is crucial
But our responses so much more,
For if you react to adversity
Your life will be more secure,
Than if you just roll over
Bleating about having no luck.
So if not standing your own ground
You may regret your lack of pluck.

--ooOoo--

Banana split

I knew it could be a difficult day
When my banana was hard to peel,
Maybe trying not to come apart
So I respected how it must feel.

For most of us from time to time,
Must be like the banana resisting
Being split open and vulnerable,
And no more life existing.

So we put up our resistance
And protect soft spots inside,
Though at times like a banana
We are completely open wide,
And expose our inner self
We don't always want seen.
Not necessarily in a bad way
Just what's behind our screen.

For certainly I have traits
I don't want put out on show.
Though nothing that's unpleasant,
Just things that make me glow
With pride or sometimes anger,
That I'd rather were unknown.
So if I can keep my outer skin
My cover won't be blown.

Thus mostly it is just a game
We all play in an attempt to fit,
Nicely in everyday surroundings
And not be a banana split.

--ooOoo—

Home Comforts

You must really count your blessings
I do that each and every day,
For there's always someone worse off
No matter what you think or say!

We live closely in our own world
So don't see much else around,
And very little affects us here
Thus we sleep safe and sound.

No war now overshadows us
Earthquake, drought or heavy weather.
In fact if we get deep heavy snow
There's panic running hell for leather!

We have no major killing diseases
Of course cancer threatens us all,
But that's a worldwide problem too
Thus our health concerns are small.
Well apart that is from obesity
That will be the new fatal killer,
Unless people stop eating fast food
And go easy on their stomach filler.

Laurie Wilkinson

We live closely in our own world
So don't see much else around,
And very little affects us here
Thus we sleep safe and sound.

So rest safely in your beds tonight,
For it's only you that cause distress
And shock waves in your tranquil pond,
So why would we settle for less!

--ooOoo--

Days

We count our time and mark it
By the number of our days,
Although this can be deceiving
For they're spent in different ways.
With some people doing nothing
Content to watch the world go by,
But others work or fill their hours
So for them their days will fly.

Though time will always beat us
As like the tide it never waits,
So before we're mindful of it
We are at those proverbial gates!

So looking back at times past
Allows our yesterdays to arrange
Thoughts some will say are foolish
For those days we cannot change.
But perhaps looking back is prudent
With its memories and teaching,
To review and maybe smile
At our actions so far reaching.

Thus if those past times are sad
It is best not to mope or dwell,
As we can take lessons forward
So may prevent another hell,
Which perhaps befell our lot
Whether ours or others fault,
But if the learning has gone in
We should not again get caught.

Another concern for some folks
Is having ambitious dreams,
That can change days into nights
And a life not what it seems.
But enjoy and embrace such thoughts
Even if your body they do tire,
For it's a very strong belief
That we need dreams to aspire.

So there is the quandary of life
No matter what you think or say,
For we live in the here and now
And must fulfil the present day.

--ooOoo--

Better or Worse

The years that pass will change us all
For many better ways, some worse.
Struggling through life's many trials
We will be tested, chapter and verse.

People we meet in life may cheat
And not turn out as we perceived,
But if we challenge or call them out
They'll protest, and be aggrieved.
For we've not measured up for them
All they needed to take from us,
Thus we must stand there as accused
Denied speech, or to make a fuss!

So the time that's passing changes all
But if faltering we can be condemned.
Though our good points are overlooked
And our errors we did not amend.

Many disputes are caused by love
And disagreements as to who is best.
So friendships that stood many years
Will struggle to survive this test!

If someone once close can succeed
When your friend and mate just fails,
A jealousy and sourness may arise
So friendship poisoned, just derails.

Our money is a tricky source of change
When wasted, stolen, lost or gained.
For everyone could make their pile
And those who didn't, say they refrained
To take the opportunities that they had
Because to achieve all is so simple,
But of course didn't take their chance
So hate disfigures, like a rash or pimple.

Thus life will salute all those who stand
Unbeaten, without change, so sincere,
Through all ravages of life upon them.
But maybe not so good as they appear.
For little temptations may have wrought
Some small dents in their gold exterior!
And denied too vigorously if not true
Prove that they actually are inferior!

--ooOoo--

Please Forgive My Warts

Please forgive the warts that disfigure me
For they've been accumulated over time,
That wasn't always too nice or good
As I journeyed from my prime.

For some experiences were quite cruel
And left splinters and open sores,
That festered despite any courage
As I fought those life-time wars.

So however hard you try to smile
When you churn and burn inside,
The adventurers on life's roads
Have nowhere safe to hide.

So although you can't see my warts
I can assure you that they're there,
But for those who won't see the scars
There is relief they don't need to care,
Or pretend that they just can't see
The countless troubles of mankind.
For when it comes to helping out,
Many pretend they're blind.

But for me I find it very hard
To ignore or pass by distress,
Which probably added to my warts
Though again, you might not guess.

For we are always asking each other
If we're alright, but don't really give a jot,
And the reply nobody wants to hear
Is someone saying, no they're not!

--ooOoo--

Secrets

Every one of us has secrets
And little stories that somehow,
Come creeping from our memories
To be confronted here and now.
For as warned by a great poet
Of tangled webs when we deceive,
That when considered in later life
We scarcely can believe.

But we cannot change our history
Of things we've said and done,
However much we would like to
As before it was just fun,
Or maybe a bit more than that
Involving both illicit touch and kiss.
Which although fantastic at the time
Much later it seems remiss.

For we could have been caught out
If involved in some emergency,
That made it very hard to explain
Why not where we said we'd be.
As covert activities can go wrong
However calculating or vain
We attempt to be when involved,
With money, sex or gain.

Thus temptations may have won
However much you bluster or deny,
As all humans have their weaknesses
No matter if strong, brazen, or shy.
So the most unlikely people fail
To resist personal gain, sex or cash,
And in some cases involve them all
If dreams and passions flash.

So simplistically the bible tells
A non sinner to cast the first stone,
Which would certainly ensure now
That no one would be alone,
To hurl the stone or missile
If it meant pointing a finger.
As on hallowed, non guilty land
None of us could linger.

But that won't prevent most people
From desperately trying to save,
Their face, or those of loved ones
As they take secrets to the grave.

Though life often has the last call
And somehow finds things out,
Leaving the credibility of that person
Tarnished, and in great doubt!

--ooOoo--

You Made Your Bed

You made your bed so lie in it,
As the old-time saying goes.
In a quite damning exclamation
Aimed, and thus delivered at those,
Who maybe took a chance
About a decision or a choice.
Sometimes leading to heartache
Or perhaps occasions to rejoice.

So possibly the receiver of,
The "well you made your bed",
Perhaps felt very pressurised
And only took a chance instead,
Of sticking to a safer place
That then really appealed.
But a chance had to be taken on,
Though not what it revealed.

Now some people make decisions
Against all sensible argument,
When going out on chancy limbs
In a steadfast manner of intent,
Possibly to shock or make a show
Against accepted points of view,
So they are prepared take blame
For opposite things they do.

But while we salute their bravery
Trying to cock snoops at convention.
If going wrong for them at the end
There's no sympathy for intention.

And although that's mostly the case,
Some people have to take a chance.
Because it's the lesser of two evils
Which makes them take a stance,
That may seem on the surface
A choice of how making their bed.
But in some extreme situations
If they don't they might be dead.

Because our world isn't totally safe
And terrorism and criminals thrive,
So at times simple innocent folks
Have to take risks to stay alive.
And if looks like they deserve trouble
For making of their metaphoric bed,
Give them the benefit of doubt
And having to listen to their head.

--ooOoo--

Awake

Oh why am I fully awake?
When the world around me sleeps,
So what is going on in my head
That from my slumber keeps?

I was tired when I went to bed
With my eyes trying to close.
But I still awoke very early
Which started off my woes.
Because I just couldn't return
To that lovely land of sleep,
With many thoughts disturbing me
And from any peace did keep.

So at first I just lay there quietly
As my mum had said, was resting.
But the failure to drop off again
My agitated mood was testing.

For I was now needing to resort
To my tried and tested ploys,
Like a hot milky drink, and music
And a return to sleeping joys.
But sadly all attempts failed
As I couldn't get back off again,
Which started to cause concern
In case I went insane.

Thus another tactic was needed
In attempt not to shout and curse.
For I just started to write again,
And produced this piece of verse!

--ooOoo--

Fake

Some things that we meet in life
Are just fake and counterfeit.
Though we may not always know,
For they can sorely test our wit.
Whether friends, gems or paintings
The results are just as bad,
But for me the worst is with people
As I find that so very sad.

For there's not much else so tragic
Or debilitating to us all.
As when somebody lures you on,
Purposely to make you fall,
Into a false and cruel game
Where only the genuine lose.
Because of crafty, evil cunning
Contrived by a callous ruse,
To get you to open up
Giving all your secrets out.
So they can be used against you
And they will, without a doubt!

For some new affections are a trap
Set by the uncaring and the smart,
Who are completely void of conscience
And will probably have no heart.

But don't be too down heartened
For these manipulators are rare,
And you can meet many honest folk
Who can make your heart a pair.
Thus just be very careful
About all the moves you make,
For if your guts give out a warning
Then they probably are a fake.

--ooOoo--

Sleep Perchance?

We all love and need our sleep
Perchance to dream as the bard said,
So just relax and prepare to rest
When you put yourself to bed.

For sleep they say, is a great healer
And recharges both body and mind,
To feel refreshed in a healthy way
Maybe to solve problems too, I find.
For we're also advised in life
To "sleep on" a decision I hear,
But whether this is true or not
In the morning things seem clear.

Thus allow yourself to drift away
And to slip into a world of dreams,
Maybe to caress those hidden thoughts
So all will not be as it seems.
Then allow the visions of your deep
To take you soaring to the moon,
In a fluttering of warm sensations
You awaken from much too soon.

So just relax and prepare to escape
When laying down to sleep,
For if you can lose yourself in peace
Great councils you will keep.

--ooOoo--

My Chair

I think most of us have that special place
And that is "my chair" and where I sit,
Because no other seating area at home
Will be as good as that one perfect fit,
Of great comfort and for watching T V
So generally settles you at your ease,
From the cut and thrust of daily life
As your own throne needs no squeeze.

For it has taken the form of your body
Just like a cooking mould for a cake,
To give you that feeling of relaxed joy
And allows each move you make.

So whilst most household sizes vary
On the number of the family group,
Many probably have a favourite perch
If all gathered in the domestic coop.
Though I will venture to be quite bold
In that very few will change their places,
Because however much we do deny it
Most people have favourite spaces.

Now just to add a little more intrigue
Regarding folks living alone and free,
To just go and sit wherever they want
But choose only one special chair to be
Their regular seat without any thought,
When they return home to sit and rest.
For no matter how many free places
Only that "my chair" passes the test.

So I guess I have followed my parents
Who both always sat in the same chair,
To settle and relax in comfortable mode
Without stopping to think or even care.
Therefore I will happily just suggest
Continuing where we put our backside,
When needing to clock off from the day
So I'll relax in "my chair" with pride.

--ooOoo--

Reflections

PAST

Reflective Views

Your reflection in a mirror
May give you some idea,
Of how you look to others
Although not always sincere.

But a photo can also give
A permanent reflective view,
Though if it was posed for
May not be genuine and true.

For we need neutral opinion
On unguarded moments where,
We react to everyday events
As the world stops to stare.

--ooOoo--

Laurie Wilkinson

Where?

Where have all my years gone
And can I please get them back?
I promise that I won't waste them
For I never let sad times stack
Up too highly in my world,
In those years of mine now past.
And I nearly always enjoyed myself
I guess why time went so fast.

So where have those years gone
Along with so many great days?
For I can still vividly remember
The songs and music that plays,
Like a magical memory jukebox
Rewinding much love and fun,
As they bring back situations
Where all was said and done.

Oh I can recall so many people
Sadly though some have gone,
Though their days are remembered
When they danced and faces shone,
From disco lights and silhouettes
Or maybe it was too much drink.
But that was in the distant past
Which makes me stop to think,
Just where have my years gone?
For it doesn't seem that long,
When my features were pristine
Like some newly written song.

Now as I look very fondly back
Over all those years I've had,
And people met and places seen
With more happier days than sad,
I feel my lifetime has stretched
Across many a stunning sunset,
But I hope for more to come
As I'm not ready to go just yet!

--ooOoo--

Laurie Wilkinson

Too Late

You never know what you have
Until you've lost it or it's gone.
Well according to the old saying
About someone who always shone
On your world and just for you,
But you no longer have them now
Or something you didn't value,
So too late for any vow.

For they may go to pastures new
Or on a new lover might decide.
And leave you trying to find them
Should they run off and hide.
Like Joni Mitchel's famous song
And line on something now gone,
Only then noticed and missed
After the event, just like a con.

Or perhaps it was a possession
That broke, or it got lost,
So now mourning its absence
You begin to count the cost,
For not recognising the value
Of this item or a person's trait,
And their intrinsic worth to you,
That you recognised too late.

So "too late" could be an epitaph
On many relationships that died,
But perhaps could have been saved
If both involved parties had tried,
A lot harder to make things work
On a relationship truly great,
But unknown or appreciated
Until sadly much too late.

--ooOoo--

Laurie Wilkinson

Past Echoes

There is a teardrop on the table
From the whispers of the past,
For all the dreams and plans
That somehow did not last.

Despite all, you've emerged now
Out from those mists of time,
Saw the rivers that contained you
And the hills you could not climb.

So you made your way regardless
Of the pitfalls and the traps,
And settled in your castle
With scarce a dip or lapse.

Maybe your destiny is different
From what you'd hoped it would be,
But looking back from now
At that time you could not see
Without the gift of foresight
Just how everything would end.
So thoughts of could've, should have
Are now just scars to mend.

Of course it could be different
From how it's all turned out,
Knowing then just what would happen
We would succeed without a doubt.
But life never is that simple
When the answers can be seen,
So we would make new errors
After the old ones we redeem.

--ooOoo--

The Pool and the Leaves

There's a camp site by my French place
With a small, round swimming pool,
That gets leaves dropping in it
Which is not too good at all.
So every morning of each day
The site manager would get them out.
Which was appreciated by swimmers,
And of that there is no doubt.

He also used to maintain the camp
Making sure everything was clean,
Not just because it was his job
But so it looked nice when seen.
Though sadly he is no longer here
For cruel cancer took him away,
And those leaves are still dropping
But the pool gets cleared each day.

So as I pass, or sit with a drink
At the site bar that's just nearby,
I often get to wonder about life
Which can often make us cry.
For the man who cleaned the pool
Was nowhere near my years,
Yet was removed from life early
Condemning his family to tears.

Now many of us will leave things
That occupy ourselves and time,
And when we have left the world
We hope memories remain sublime.
So for me it's my words and poems
About love, life and she who grieves,
Over things still here without us
Like the man who cleared the leaves.

--ooOoo--

Laurie Wilkinson

Imagination

It's so easy to sit and dream
Bringing wonders all around,
As you create great events
Then make them truly found.

Well maybe truth in your world
But not one that accepts a lie,
For imagined dreamy events
Won't fit however you try.

Though maybe past memories
On which incidents are caught,
Possibly did happen back then
But not exactly as you thought.
For memories can always seem
To deceive us in some ways,
Which will all cause confusion
About those long past days!

But that is natural enough
And we can be lured into error,
With events from long years back
That no longer cause us terror,
Making them much more likely
To confound and dull our wit.
So we will evoke imagination
To make those memories fit.

--ooOoo--

Laurie Wilkinson

Heartfelt

A positive mind yields a happy heart
For troubles come, and some go slow.
But if you are steadfast in your way,
   You can help any heartaches go.

For all of us will have challenges,
And must do our very best to meet
With strongest resolve we can find,
Or get knocked right off our feet,
By seismic shocks that shake you
And possibly cause you many tears.
Though if you tackle these heroically
You may have better future years.

For a positive mind yields a happy heart
And helps make worries seem smaller,
Thus meet them in a courageous way
And you certainly will walk taller.

For I feel I'm living proof of this
Being a very optimistic man.
Though I have had many troubles too
But met them the best way I can,
For even if I lost sometimes
I always stood back up again,
Which certainly was best for me
Although of course I felt the pain.

So onwards in life and upwards
We must make our merry way,
Because even if sad times prevail
We can still fight another day.

--ooOoo--

Laurie Wilkinson

Blind Alleys

The sands of time will educate
Just what we should have done,
But these lessons are of no use
However quick we run.

The past is gone and can't be changed
However much we'd like to,
Forget, erase and put all right
So it rests at ease inside you.

So try to forget or come to terms
With things that don't sit light,
Upon a conscience shouting out
The things you can't make right.

Mistakes made, or spiteful words
May reappear and haunt,
An awakened or sleepless soul
That bad memories will flaunt.

There's a private calling inner self
That speaks louder in the dark,
Of uncertainties that grow
Bright from the smallest spark.

The very stoutest heart and frame
Will wilt from past torment,
Unless a covenant you make
Before your time is spent.

Words spoken and dreams made
At a time your ideas leapt,
Seemed all right and proper then
So them now you must accept!

--ooOoo--

Laurie Wilkinson

Moment in Time

The world spins on its axis
Night darkens the light of day,
Summer follows winter and spring
Our times were made that way.

Yet we go on in our existence
Even if we want to or not,
For however much we fight it
We mostly have the life we've got.
For as we continue on our road,
Days will come that bring our turn.
To have some suffering to bear,
From which we need to learn.

For as our loved ones die on us
Others will come as we see them go.
Replaced by babes newly born,
In natures continuous flow.
So enjoy what you have now
For as long as you possibly can,
Because there is no certainty
Of the time scale given to man.

Waiting for exactly the right time
To do all that you want to do,
May catch you out very badly
And be totally denied to you.
Thus best appreciate it all now
Even if the truth hurts and numbs,
For however hard to accept it
Sometimes tomorrow never comes.

--ooOoo--

Laurie Wilkinson

Inner Tears

I have heard that when you cry
Tears are words hearts can't express,
But whatever reason for their visit
It can be a sign of great distress.

Of course there are tears of joy
And some of laughter in a form,
But none can seem as heart-rending
As anguish riding out a storm.

Tears of grief or frustration perhaps
Are streaming down your face,
You should not be ashamed of this
As it really is no disgrace.
For those who cry are often caring
And so let their passions free,
Unlike blank faced stone hearts
That other people's woe can't see.

We can cry at the world's sadness
Or what it has all done to us,
So some will weep out openly
Others cry with much less fuss.
But however you shed your tears
When pain's too much to bear,
It just proves you have empathy
And that you do, really care.

So pucker up, let yourself go
Express emotions and your views,
For if you cannot manage this
You live a life that has no clues.

--ooOoo--

People Places

People and places from your past
Are no longer there, or the same.
So will make you notice more
The years you couldn't tame.

People known from distant days
Maybe won't still be around.
So you must indulge old friends
Before you too run aground.

Places where you knew each stone
Will now soon lose you in a trice,
And even finding a familiar part
Will still make you look twice,
Because memories will play tricks
On what you thought you knew,
And many a place or person now
Seems different from your view.

People known from distant days
Maybe won't still be around.
So you must indulge old friends
Before you too run aground.

So going back where you've been
May not be for the very best,
As these places may disturb you
If they've not survived times test.

But people are somewhat different
Always worth a nostalgic greet,
For though they may have changed
It will be good for you to meet,
And share those long-gone times
Where you both ran alongside,
Each other with your experiences
From which you should not hide!

--ooOoo--

Laurie Wilkinson

Your Story

Everyone has their personal story
And it may seem trivial or immense,
To an unforgiving world audience
Maybe observing from their fence.

But if a story appears insignificant
To the owner it is paramount,
Whilst maybe feeling overshadowed
Their story is the only one to count.
For each individual lifetime story
However mundane or small it seems,
Will for each and every one of us
Project innermost hopes and dreams.

Although the telling of this life
Varies from one person to the next,
With often very mixed reaction
Depending on the spoken text.
For how this life is delivered
To perceptive receiving ears,
Can be with growing interest
Or maybe boring them to tears.

But of course there are people
Who believe that their every word,
And most miniscule life event
Is just waiting to be heard,
By rapturous, riveted audiences
Taking every little fact down,
When really laughing deep inside
And regarding them as a clown.

So be very careful with your story
And how you present all about you,
For by far the greatest achievement
Is if others speak of what you do.

--ooOoo--

Cradle to the Grave

A lilting voice from the past
That will affect you like no other.
Bringing love and goose bumps too,
For it can only be your mother.

The one who always from your birth
Stood by you with no quaking,
Though inside she cried bitter tears
If bad decisions you were making,
Or was given cause to be upset
At your failure to return the love,
Which will always be too late
After she is taken to live above.

For a mother always looks with pride
At your first shaky steps to walk,
Across your rocky paths in life
Since she first helped you to talk.
Thus had also been there for you
From that cradle to the grave,
Watching out for all those dangers
As your soul she tried to save.

So when others reject and doubt you
Your doting mother will be there,
To ensure she can protect you
With unconditional loving care,
That first began when as a child
You needed succour and a kiss,
Given with uncomplaining lips
You will always sorely miss.

A lilting voice from the past
You will remember all your years,
Though may not always appreciate
Until her passing brings your tears.
So while you have her, be ever nice
To your solid embracing fir,
Who whatever heartbreak you cause
Will still put you first, before her.

--ooOoo--

Laurie Wilkinson

Reflections

TRAGIC

Accident Report

There has been an accident
At such and such a place and road.
An everyday announcement we hear
But for some the world will explode.
As spouses or family members
Or even perhaps best friends,
Could be caught up in the smash
And for some their life ends.

Thus for thousands of people each year
The accident news that was read,
Would have devastating consequences
Of serious injuries, with some dead.
Because these accidents that we hear of
Happen each and every day,
With lives changed drastically forever
Despite how hard you beg and pray.

So what causes all of these crashes
Often on roads that are mostly straight?
Well it could be drink or drugs,
Or simply someone just can't wait
Before risking a tricky manoeuvre,
Whilst some will be on their phone
But whatever is the cause
Someone could now be alone.

Of course as humans we make mistakes
In judging distances, times and speeds.
Maybe just not seeing clearly
Can be as little as it needs,
To cause life to be snuffed out
And all of us can be guilty too.
Although most won't admit to this
The facts will prove it's true.

So best to take some time out
To consider how we drive,
For with less speed and drinking
Many more people will stay alive,
Or not spend their life on crutches
Maybe with a disfigured face,
So try your best to ensure
An accident is not your disgrace.

--ooOoo--

Living Well

If you're thirsty you may go to the well
To quench your thirst with a drink.
And you may do it automatically
Without ever stopping to think,
About how the water got there
Or the need to put something back,
Because the water may soon run dry
If the well is allowed to crack.

For in our world little comes for free
Although plenty will live for this,
By taking out everything they can
And giving help requests a miss.
For they are too busy taking all
It's possible to get lazy hands upon,
Ensuring when it's pay back time
They'll be well and truly gone.

So for us in a concerned majority
Is the need take care of our well
And other gifts passed on to us,
As they are not ours to waste or sell.
When the sacrifice of many others
Gave them up without a cost,
Only a big responsibility of trust
To see they are never lost.

Thus this commitment is now ours
To appreciate and protect this wealth,
Of the things we may take for granted
All the time they're in good health.
But just a little thought and effort
Will see our gifts all safely supplied,
And to know our drinking well is flowing
Will meet our wish after we've died.

--ooOoo—

Hand of God

Scenic beauty, sweet fresh air
All you could wish for, it was all there,
For one more moment, then it was gone
When the coward set off another bomb.

Smoke and flames, cries and screams
Another end to countless dreams,
A place of wonder to melt all hearts
Was now a horror of body parts!

All be praised, his god is served
The dead just got what they deserved,
For not praying the same as those
Who blew them up and burnt their clothes.

Some strange god, that death he asks
From his army with their bloody tasks,
That spreads out terror, fear and dread
And victories measured by the dead.

Again you pray, your day is won
Religion spread by your smoking gun,
It is honour you want, your way is best,
Go tell the man with his shattered chest.

Little children, babes in arms
Now lie slaughtered with no more charms,
You say it is vengeance, we had done wrong
So we must suffer your sick death song.

It is peace you wish, and to make us sure
You continue to kill, and make more war,
Until we learn, and have passed the test
That your gentle, loving god is the best.

--ooOoo--

Someone Says Goodbye

See how quick we can be gone
And the world will blink and carry on,
With another soul out the exit door
As we wonder what life is for.

But there must be more for us than this
A racing heart and a loving kiss,
While our struggles and an uphill climb
Take our words and makes them mime.

Mothers, fathers, siblings and friends
We are all these before our ends,
But what of this when we are to go
What will change and who will know?

See how quick we can be gone
And the world will blink and carry on,
So we may learn how hard they try
When someone has to say goodbye.

Laughing, crying, bitter sweet years
That give us joy, or shed our tears,
And looking back from an ageing eye
Condemning those that would not try,
To ever give, or leave their mark
On a wasted life without a spark,
As for them it was all much too hard
They passed on by, never played a card.

See how quick we can be gone
And the world will blink and carry on,
With daily tasks that must be done
Or problems causing us to run.

But wait, a lesson will be taught
From those who died, but valiant fought,
To spend more time with those that care
Not granted! Who said life was fair?
So as we hear their struggling breath
As they slide towards impending death,
See how quick we can be gone
And the world might blink and carry on.

But some things can make life worthwhile
Just leave a little of your style,
To sprinkle out and upward fly
When our turn comes to say goodbye.

--ooOoo--

Game to Lose

Your game of life is often played
In front of the watching crowd,
Who see your each and every move
As you stand small, or very proud.

So the fence sitters will only watch
How others cope with their game.
And decrying all those who've lost
Whilst jealous of the victors fame.

For if you won't take a part in life
You can deride and mock at will,
All those who try to do their best
To enjoy life, and so they'll fulfil.

So that's why I have strongly felt
It's far better to have tried and lost.
For if you won't compete or try
You'll much later count your cost,
Of just cowardly sitting at the side,
Never taking any risk or chance.
Making you a lonely, boring case,
And not worth a second glance!

But by getting stuck in having a go
It's just possible you may win out.
And that must be so much better
Than not to know a winners shout.

So our cosy spectators of the world
Will always rue not being brave,
And missed the warmth of joining in
Thus taking a sadness to their grave!

--ooOoo--

Stain of Shame

Near three thousand went to work
Though none would make it back,
As they would all be the victims
Of a sick cowardly attack.

Without any warning from the skies
And two huge towers did remove.
Though left a bigger stain of shame,
Of which no god could approve.

Many a madman in history charged
With a massive sword a wielding,
But it takes a special psychotic mind
To steer planes into a building!

A tremor was felt across humanity
We knew that evil had been done,
But their bitter, sickly souls were less,
Than their smoke that hid the sun.

Near three thousand went to work
Though none would make it back,
They would all be the victims
Of a sick, cowardly attack.

With towers burning there is no escape
Trapped up high from crowds around,
The only choice was manner of death
To burn, choke, or hit the ground.

There was time though, with technology
For tragic folk to phone their kin,
And heartrending love and goodbyes
Only compound their killer's sin.

They said the world couldn't be the same
After this cruel act of desecration,
But the spirit of good and righteousness
Is built on a very strong foundation.

Near three thousand went to work
Though none would make it back,
They would all be the victims
Of a sick, cowardly attack.

So time has passed into history now
That blackest day of days.
The world moves on now as it must,
But contempt and disgust still stays,
For those whose simplistic minds
Were twisted to an act of hate,
Upon unsuspecting innocents
Who walked like heroes to their fate!

--ooOoo--

Not That Kind of Time

With stealth and cruelty the years go by
Casting spells on both body and mind,
So that we wither and our frailties form
Thus we realise, time's not that kind.

Our resisting brain cells and lively wit
Dispute any damage is being done,
So you still believe you are fit and well
When in truth you can barely run.
But is it wrong to live a white lie?
You're still young and everything works,
For the real truth will slowly seep in
So that doubts and uncertainty lurks.

Going back over time, you now see it all.
The things you did, or should have tried,
For however much you want to catch up
You can't do this when you've died.

The march of the years won't be stopped
Whatever actions you try to pursue.
For once you did things to kill time,
But that time is now killing you!

With stealth and cruelty the years go by
Casting spells on both body and mind,
So that we wither and our frailties form
Thus we realise, time's not that kind.

They say time and tides wait for no man
Though we can do things as they release,
But do not squander or spoil the years
Or you will lose your inner peace.
So maybe best to make a covenant now
As your body loses all strength and vigour,
For the secret of youth and endless life
Is a solution we are yet to figure.

--ooOoo--

Days of Tears

Days of tears will come for everyone
But for some will last much longer,
Depending on those choices made
Are you weaker, or lots stronger?

For we're living today, decisions past
When maybe didn't count to ten,
So whether we like it now or not
We must accept life as decided then.
But possibly in previous times
Those options did seem right,
So now you must live with them
However hard they come to bite.

A wrong lover or chance declined
May seem sad in the here and now,
But reflecting back to decision time
You were so certain of your vow.
Perhaps to be childless did appeal
Rocking to your very own way,
But in days of flowing tears now
Accept your loneliness today.

Laurie Wilkinson

For days of tears will always come
With regrets, and perhaps sorrow,
So best to count every blessing now
Or you may cry at each tomorrow.

--ooOoo--

Open Prison

Prisons don't all have bars
Like Mandela's cell so cruel.
For even with open spaces
Some confinements can still rule
The very limits of your scope
And any foray you'd like to make.
So restricted in your freedom
You feel your heart will break.

Seeing just everything you want
Or would like so much to do,
Can crack your very being
When it's all denied to you.
For if you try to journey out
Those chains won't let you go,
Yanking you back severely
With a more than physical blow.

For a soul that is so tortured
By wishes it can't enjoy,
Will be heavy, dark and rotten
From desires it can't employ.
So must look forlornly about
At scenes that appeal so much,
But remain unfulfilled and empty
From attractions it can't touch.

Laurie Wilkinson

Thus imprisoned in a carcass
But though dead, will still breathe,
This soul will know real anguish
Caused by restraints that peeve.

--ooOoo--

Fortitude

The shrieking wind shook off the hand
Desperately clinging to the rail,
And threatened to flatten him
For fighting was to no avail,
As weakened frame and battered mind
Could offer no more defence,
Against the elements bombardment
So now resistance made no sense.

But a defiant spark was remaining
While a strong will said hold on,
And struggle to the bitter end
When all hope has finally gone.
Because man has a deep inner will
That can achieve huge success,
When all has appeared hopeless
And seemed an impossible mess.

But what is it that drives us on
Like the intrepid case as above?
Well I believe it is our fine spirit
And a considered belief that love
Can help us overcome diversity
And everything that life can throw.
But obviously there are times
When we just have to let go.

So meanwhile we can take a lead
From courageous exploring heroes,
Who forged new paths and discoveries
So that everywhere man now goes,
He has the lessons on fortitude
Taught by Trojans from the past,
Who used love and determination
To teach how to make it last.

--ooOoo--

Missing

Most of us will have loved ones
That we enjoy hugging and kissing,
But sometimes life can become hard
If a special one just goes missing.
Because you may not have a clue
Of situations untoward or wrong,
But concerns and fears may escalate
If a disappearance goes on too long.

As over two hundred thousand people
Just go off and disappear each year,
And that's one adult in five hundred
Who give their families cause to fear,
For their safety and well-being
When having a personal nightmare,
That they could be suffering alone
And feel nobody seems to care.

Though most people who go missing
Seem to very soon get safely back,
But others can be away for decades
And in long years all contact they lack,
Leaving families worried and afraid
Of that door knock they dread to hear,
Telling them their missing relative
Will no longer be coming near.

For sadly many never will return
Or complete a suicide they planned,
Thus a bewildered and guilty feeling
Leaves friends and family damned,
By a failure of real understanding
Of why no cry for help was heard.
Nor any noticed behaviour change,
And in fact they never said a word.

Now it can really only be imagined
The level of pain and anguish felt,
By usually decent and loving family
Of treasured relatives who melt
Away into a world full of uncertainty
With cameras and security everywhere,
But still fail to find or solve a mystery
Why the missing leave folks who care.

--ooOoo--

One in Three

Love and laughter may sprinkle around
With no real problems for you and me,
But we must always be aware of the fate
That will befall every one in three.

For our lives can change in a trice
When the world sends us a test,
To deal with tragedy, failure or loss
When we are forced to do our best,
To keep our chins up and smile
And face the world with fragile pride,
That may fool many, and maybe you
Until you realise you're dying inside.

As a blackness so dark falls all over you
With no pinprick of light in your pit,
So you blunder about and don't even try
Whilst every sinew begs you to quit,
And perhaps shuffle off this mortal coil
That right now seems most appealing,
For even if you do try to fight back
You're overwhelmed by a darkest feeling.

Laurie Wilkinson

Where has all this come from you ask?
But in truth you may never know,
How you are reduced to anxiety tears
And constant feelings of death and woe,
That will affect many now in their lives
As if have swallowed a depressive pill,
For you have become one in the three
Who learn the trauma to be mentally ill.

--ooOoo--

The Spider and the World

The spider lurks in the shadows
And then its web will spin,
Waiting for the world to arrive
Before naively going in.

The world too will spin around
As we mere mortals live our days,
Trying to understand everything
In so many different ways.
With some things we succeed
But others will prove too much,
For that's the way of a complex world
And what we never get to touch.

Meanwhile the hermit like spider
Sits patiently in its thread,
Awaiting for the blind unwary
Who very soon will be dead.
Stuck and trapped quite helpless
Condemned to a gruesome fate,
In the cruel fangs of that spider
Or maybe killed by its mate.

So perhaps there is a comparison
Between the spider's web and man,
Who in their very different ways
Just get by the best they can.

With one sitting in a subtle trap
As for victims it quietly waits.
While we in our world twirl in frenzy
And dread to hear what fates
Or misfortune will befall us,
With nerve ends all stretched taut,
Before blundering through our lives
And in webs of deceit get caught.

--ooOoo--

Appendix

Kind compliments and feedback to me on my poetry now increases as I continue to write and produce more books, number thirteen now, but it still recounts that many people like to work out the meanings of my poems for themselves, or even attach their own personal experiences and thoughts as they resonate with them.

I think that is truly wonderful, but for other folks who like to seek my reasons and explanations for aspects of my poems, please review my comments below.

As I tend to write spontaneously and often on subjects that have really emoted me, I will mostly "nail my thoughts in", so most of the themes are quite clear or self explanatory.

However the poems listed in this appendix below are the less obvious topics and thoughts, but please attach any personalisation or special meaning that they have for you individually, because I will feel really honoured if you do!

Across the Way:
That life isn't always fair but must be lived whatever you feel

Recycle Plant:
On people's thoughts and ideas to better themselves, but lack courage to try

Blind Alleys:
To learn from our life experiences

Better or Worse:
Judgemental people forgetting their own transgressions

People Places:
Don't miss out on seeing old friends

Stain of Shame:
Condemnation of 9/11 terror attack, and its repercussions on people's lives

Game to Lose:
Ignorance and loss of "none triers" who criticise others attempts

Voice Within:
Encouragement to confront your fears

Pass or Fail:
Reflecting back on our decisions in life

Not That Kind of Time:
Reminder not to waste your time, or life

Days of Tears:
That we must mostly live today on our decisions from the past

Past Echoes:
For people to put any "life regrets" into perspective

Yellow Brick Code:
Parable type story advising not to betray beliefs for false goals

Alone in the Mirror:
Recognition of getting older as life goes on

The Spider and the World:
That our own little world can be very different to other peoples

Open Prison:
People can be trapped by thoughts and their lives become an imprisonment

Will:
Suggesting just how quickly life can change for us without warning

Effortless:
My take on "3 Little Pigs" story and that some folks won't contribute anything

Banana Split:
That each of us can be vulnerable, and mostly just want to fit in

Imagination:
On people making things up and then believing that they are true or real

You Made Your Bed:
Sometimes we must make "our bed in life" not how we would choose

Fragile Flame:

Recognising you can only do so much however big the
load put on you

Living Well:

To look after all we have in the world for following
generations

Hand of God:

Revulsion that religion often used as vehicle for
terrorism.

More?

I hope that you enjoyed this book
For I tried to pack lots in,
With various themes in sections
So you can choose where to begin,
And take yourself on journeys
Or if you wished to, just remain.
For I have other books out now,
Thus you can have it all again.

With poems to make you romantic
And some verses if you feel deep.
Others will make you look back on life,
Even smile when you go to sleep.

Ted and Beth will normally feature
I can hardly leave them out.
As surely they'll have new adventures,
Well of this I have no doubt!
And I will have new observations
I glean from scanning life's tree.
Take care then you are not included
When I write down what I see.

So please look at my other books
And support "Help for Heroes" too,
For all my sales donate to them
From my poems I write for you.

You can get books from my website online
And to message me direct will be fine.
With every contact listed below
Including all that you need to know,
To search for me on the Amazon club
Or just come and find me down the pub!

My other books are: -
Poetic Views of Life
MORe Poetic Views of Life
Reviews of Life in Verse
Life Scene in Verse
Life Presented in Verse
Poet Reveals All
Poet Reflects Your World
Our World in Verse
Laurie's Bundle of Poetic Humour
Tea for Two: Poetic Antics of Ted & Beth
Illuminating Verse: Rousing Poetry

My contacts: -
Email = lw1800@hotmail.co.uk
Amazon authors page= Laurie Wilkinson
Facebook page = The Psychy Poet Laurie
Wilkinson
Facebook page =Ted n Beth of Laurie the Poet
Website = www.lauriewilkinson.com

Reflections

Printed in Great Britain
by Amazon